GARDEN THEOLOGY

Sunlight on Bolivar Pond, Norfolk County, Massachusetts

"Across the silvered pond
Were deep woods without name,
For journeys into wrested sleep
And light poured, raining
Through the spring leaves,
Staining the glass of the sky."

GARDEN THEOLOGY

poems

Seán Mac Falls

Tupelo Press
North Adams, Massachusetts

Garden Theology
Copyright © 2022 Seán Mac Falls. All rights reserved.

Library of Congress Control Number: 2022938497

ISBN: 978-1-946482-77-8

Cover and text designed by Allison O'Keefe

Cover art: Odilon Redon, "Figure Under a Blossoming Tree,"
digitally remastered edition, courtesy of Art Market America.
Used with permission.

First edition: August 2022.

Tupelo Press
P.O. Box 1767, North Adams, Massachusetts 01247
(413) 664–9611 / editor@tupelopress.org /
www.tupelopress.org

Tupelo Press is an award-winning independent literary press
that publishes fine fiction, nonfiction, and poetry in books
that are a joy to hold as well as read. Tupelo Press is a registered
501(c)(3) nonprofit organization, and we rely on public support
to carry out our mission of publishing extraordinary work that
may be outside the realm of the large commercial publishers.
Financial donations are welcome and are tax deductible.

Contents

Sonnet of Morning

Before the wings and spring of words,
Were cradle-held in a cloud of sleep,
Soft footfalls to hear ourselves turning
And ever new dreams were lofty keys,
We could not see the frost branching
And winter never was, nor winds cold,
In our temple eyes, the sun crowning
Imbued visions, fine as woven gold,
Draped in silks so rare, spun spinning,
To hear the birds sing in ears blossom,
For the very first time, true beginnings
And the flower's colour never forgotten,
All is mourning now—song, sings singer,
To morn, to wake, dream, dreams dreamer.

Rose Alone with Crow

In straps, of wire saplings,
Becomes one wild rose.
Alone in the dawn,
A solitary crow knows
That this is beauty,
Greater than his own
Shiny black robe.
Impossibly regal,
Red as a scarlet wail,
A siren, among all
The greens and yellows
Of a meadow, of the entire
World, is the rose, above those,
Especially the bleak, envious
Crow, latched to a branch
As scaly and gnarled as his soul,
Blacker than eternal night,
Beside the shining light
Of the rightly charmed
Wild rose,
Alone.

      Sorry is the crow—
Most of all unmatched, strikingly
To long flame of chalk-faced moon,
Rides in airs, misbegotten, makes
Desolate cries, of wounding caws,
Self-inflicted, so, somehow seems
Unalive, tarred, undead as smoke,
His fettered, black, unfeathering

Eyes. Not like the blooming spark
And flash of the stunning, runner,
Unbeaten, indomitable, shocking,
Wild rose, unmired by bramble,
Wood nor motley thorn of bush,
A star of life, razor cut, blistering,
Free, this spirited, bloody heart,
Set, a rage, on jagged leaf.
In tangled straps of green wire saplings,
A rose is even more a rose, next to crow.

Ode to the Otter

River gift, flowing upstream and down
Cresting with the bumpy waters' tow,
Slick as an eel, you move and fro to play,
Warm in the gleaming sun that rides
With you each day,

                    you have shone, great
Knowledge of salmon, found the pearl
In the dark mussel, bend as even light
Must, piercing the waters of the under-
World, lording the fey, riparian borders,
Like a God.

Hawk Over Hill

Etched in smoke, burnished by olden sun,
The runner grasses wave below into maze,
For eyes in cloud to clutch on mottled vermin,
Higher in stations, a judgment for all grazer,

Pleated feathers arched in weightless stone,
Are blades as steely as any burnt ploughman's
And airs that break, lift hawk far into sun shone,
As quake of earth strikes up a still-haired louse,

For blades of green shall call, bleed in grasses
And whisper will shout, downing smallest might,
Tiny beasts who crawl among waving masses,
To hawk over hill, sheering in raiments of light.

Golden Yew

In November early, I planted a yew,
Stately, golden under Pagan moon,
It's fibers I laid into moist dark soil
And set her proudly in foggy shawl.

Needles sparking into everlasting air,
Green and gold under mantle of sun,
Wisdom staggered, grounded so fair,
Bark, red knowledge of salmons' run.

Before six moons had turned down,
Her needles fell out of limbs frozen,
By wind and rains grope, unclothed—
Sun-clad boughs now fodder to moon.

If Only She Would Die With Me

If only she would die with me—
Lying a bed on a sheet of stars,
Out of mere dark, our light set free,

Our leaves to hold in rings of tree,
Hair entwined in ocean days' hour,
If only she would die with me—

In the forest fern to rest, wake curly,
We would nest in that place so far,
Out of mere dark, our light set free,

To ever notch a simple tapestry,
Colours even sun could not mar,
If only she would die with me—

In this morning all spark wants to be,
What our bodies are joined in marking,
Out of mere dark, our light set free,

We two have eyes blistering to see
And winds that tail the song of larks,
If only she would die with me—
Out of mere dark, dear light set free.

From a Window

Scurrilous birds fly by,
To nest in the little painted
Houses left clear for them,
In awkward circles they romp
Their peculiar dramas
With tawdry wings.

Do they even witness
The skies' revolving canvas,
New masterpieces each day,
How the light shimmers
In the sparkle rays of sun,
How the golden fields,
Of vales in sighted sweep
And dance, airy etudes,
By the windfall gusts
So suddenly arising?

These visions are marks
For but few, who hear time
As it plays in stepped quartets
Of the spiraling season's song,
For the lone mercies, gifts,
To ones most gentle, merest,
Spirited eyes who gaze deftly,
Deep in sacred days,
From a window.

Smoked in Poppyhead

We drove to the wild poppy fields,
Lost and opened under felt sun,
To picnic in solemn spent wonder
And celebrate new-founded love.

Teapot rains came whispering in—
The skies blue up a clouded mood
And old mist rose in lighted eyes,
To stark sheet of uncovered brood.

We talked of one day, this day now,
As we laid with the lovelorn flowers,
A day for pictures, unmarked boxes,
How droplets grew to cold showers.

We broke down then and took leave,
Of letted time in tiers now dead—
There under cathedral glass of sun,
Our cut love smoked in poppyhead.

Named

We are born,
There is some joy
Lighting a tiled room
And the first cry echoes
In the spray, sterile hollows.
A woman simpers, flush
And torn, whimpers, softly,
Under the phosphorescences
Of terror and delight, where
A man sees his own doom
Fast approaching as he weeps
With measured happiness
And one foot by the door.

Little creature, welcome
To the world, make up
Your presence known,
Bulbous and brightly
As melons in the sun,
Waiting to be plucked
With another lover
Indifferent as you,
Arbitrary as any name
Grasped for, looked up,
Placing you into this
Home of strangers,
This globe of shadow,
Shining dimly, eyeing,
To name you quick,
Holey, somewhat
Real.

Desert King

I came to the pavilion of the big cats
And in the center was a palace ruin,
The walls were stone and feeble mortar,
The great, golden monarch was the lion.

With wisdom eyes, he gazed upon me,
I lowered my head as was my station,
He did not move, nor deign to care,
In His royal chamber I was under thrown.

I thought, you are caught my over lord,
But his stance said, these bars are scepter
And I heard him say with a long-lost roar,
"Hear my horn, I am he, the storm of Jericho."

In the palace of the mighty, indifferent king
His thundering voice crackled the lambing
Stables and even heaven closed under ceiling
Dome and I was caged when the walls fell away
And the whole, blown world, remade—a zoo.

The Searching

After childhood sleep,
Of days into dawning,
Shucked of dusted clay,
Eyes set unto fawning,

Then, the rowing began.
Shy gentle waves lulling
As it does for Everyman
Who seeks loves' culling.

In a tempest of blue sky,
I was engulfed so plain,
That time was sore to eye,
All suitors never maidens.

One true love never came,
Nor to fly as birds teeming,
Now all is shipwreck of age,
Ah, but to drown dreaming.

The Sorrow of Days

Time is teasing along with lush earth so pleasing,
The minutes of our youth are spent in toiled days
And sands are blowing the weld of our sold means,
Foundations of dust, the cries unheard, of the aged.

And then, as dream, you came from the starry skies
Blue and small as the ocean dot, forever fixed—
Reigning over the frozen, revolving moon that lies,
Dimly wakes in your fabled orbit, my fated ellipse.

Now, time tables and splits, renders me to eaves
Undone, my squandered youth was but a sad play
And I am clocked with wind, the geld of my dreams,
Had shiftless hands been more solid than my days.

Unconditional

You've asked me how can I see a future when love, in all
Its numinous beauty, is waning?
I reply, the immortal stars still shine above the veil of clouds.
You say, why are the salmon swimming to their pools
    of origin
Only to die as they spawn? Only to die?
I tell you their love is unconditional, like mine.
You ask me did the giant sequoia know it was shelter
    for the burning grasses
When they walked from the seas? I reply yes they knew.
You question me about the lofty snow cranes that fly
    over the Himalayas
And I reply by describing
How the priestly flocks, chanting on their mission, honk—
Announcing the mantle steps to the heavens.
You inquire about the elephantine manatees gracing
    the shallow banks
And wonder if the sea mermaids remember their lives
    beyond the latitudes
Of Capricorn and Cancer?
Or you've discovered in the wind a new reasoning as to why
The talons of the paired eagles lock in midair as they court?
You want to understand the nimbus garden, ocean
    slate, of Lake Titicaca
Where resides the Andean sea horse gliding above the clouds?
The whales that circle dance in unison collecting krill?
The noetic display of the birds of paradise, the songs
    of nameless creatures
Playing in the wilderness like a forgotten melody only
    lovers' lips remember?

I want to tell you that true love knows this, that life in its
Prismatic shimmer is all the myriad colours of infinite
    existence wrapped
In time to the sublime structure of white and bones.
    I must tell you
That the flower is mighty in its opening, the
    hummingbird is a sorcerer
Who needles ambrosia with vortex wings weaving his
    way to the Gods.

But I am nothing beside your disbelief which has
    arrived, before
I can even imagine the sweet awakening, like doom,
    my shell is
The iridescent hollow of the one-eyed Abalone, discarded
In the deep fathoms of the ocean pressures.

I swim the tides as you do, investigating
The endless tendril seas, and in my chest,
During the night, I woke up empty,
The only thing treasured, a golden face
Trapped inside my dreams.

— after Neruda

Leaf

In the leaf there lies—
A bold anatomy, knowing,
Veined structure exploding
Like a star, pale flash ignites
Turning into burnished gold,
Starting as dear light, loosed
Spark, coming into blessed
Being, ever before even old
Gender, a little hand growing
Open, set free before stark,
Innocence, actual as truth,
As an offering to the sun.

Body of Ocean, Milk, and Sky

Body of ocean, milk, and sky,
We are tangled in the hope of night.
The lips of the milky way, creaming us,
Stains and is tart with a taste keening;
All is creation. My meteors crash
Into your ruptured Earth. I flame
Upon your must and moisted furrows
And my toes are locked, rooted in yours.

Body of ocean, milk, and sky,
In the deserts of the day you are true
Oasis. The curves and waft of your sands
Seethe and sodden my barren plains,
Are erasing all my wandering memories
Of an endless sky and now your eyes
Are the only stars I know, and your skin;
A sheet that holds the heavens shimmering.

Body of ocean, milk, and sky,
Your breasts are the heaving of grasses
And wind, loft and laden in the rounded
Hills, a hoard of yeasty bread, bountiful,
Ripe and strange. Your hair is an endless
Savannah, your valleys are gold and honeyed
With milk, seared, filled by my penetrating sun.
In passion we play; low on earth and deep in sky.

Lovers in Morning

Sun startles the lovers who lie,
Crammed in a single bed.
Once the sun blanketed doves,
Each day a wrap for godlings
And the night was a sea of hope
For the lonely, lost, drowning.
Now the morning is a shroud
That eyes shy away from it,
They look for each other—
Out windows murky into day,
But night never really leaves,
The untouched skin breaking,
The unshared fade of breaths
Untaken, unwound fingers,
Trapped in open rooms
And light revealing,
Cold uncovered,
Lovers in morning.

Sunlight on Bolivar Pond

In early morning,
Mist revolving joys,
Everything so glorious,
The grey fox on the shores,
The great blue herons,
Light houses of dawn,
Arching into heavens,
Overlooking all souls,
Such colours by the sounds,
Lilting in the scores of clover,
Of bees notating and staffs,
Sway of staved dragonflies,
Dropped dew belled in petals
And whole world lathed
With harmonious light.

Across the silvered pond
Were deep woods without name,
For journeys into wrested sleep
And light poured, raining
Through the spring leaves,
Staining the glass of the sky,
Ordaining the stationed hearts,
Held by the still deer, who walked
On waters, wading into sun,
Each night destroyed
By freshness and rays,
The mottled waking meadows,
Green as ever growing,
More alive than old legend,
O to be a pilgrim with eyes,
Opening!

To be shy lord in the fortresses
Of fallen trees and savour such
Piney sense as rooted sassafras,
The smells of mosses and leaf,
On the shores of the painted
Turtles, shaded by lurching trees
Mushroomed over shallows, sunning,
And hear the foghorned frogs
Alerting the dark gleaming, red-
Winged blackbirds to their reeds.
Among the rocks a child
Skips, hums upon.

So breaking was the boy
In the hood of the pond,
More alive, golden, than a star,
Round that very crested shire,
In the berry vines of ripeness,
Winding marshes at play,
Where blush of wild ducks
Endlessly saunter and rooks
Dot the airs circling eternal.

Now in ages past,
After, pond enameled
So far away still sings
Of childhood to come,
For any lost soul who waits,
Beyond cries, a warble's lulling,

What songbirds might ring,
For newborns who break,
Ashed in sands of the quick,
Into some future paradise,
Births of new days dawning,
Rung through, dominions of the sun.

We Were as Downy Birds

We were as downy birds,
Sky once had names for us,
Rain pooled into faery wells,
Supernatural was our blood.

We saw each with opened eyes,
And touch was permanent as sun,
Light swooned about our keeping
And the earth was without tomb.

But time soon railed its perishments
And a star turned with pointed wind,
We lost the sun raise of innocence
And the glass of truth broke in a jar.

Now, lovers roam in the still hollows
And reminisce only on stoney banks,
A great ocean of peace was drowned
And to childish walls, a castle of sands.

Garden Proverbs . . .

1

Old Stone Wall

Lumpy fields of fox hole heaved by a harrow,
Boulders drawn, lifted on break weather stall,
Bundles of crops strewn, wall stone shrapnel,
Within lines so drawn, only a few have fallen.

2

Gates of Cloud

Coastal mist and mountains blue as ache—
Troubled waters in midair, streaming across
Such mirage of openness and tangled range,
When will the gathering skies sing me aloft?

3

The Erne and the Lamb

Little lambs gathered on the precipice,
Soft and snowy, peaceful and patching,
Their numbers change in spotting fog,
By the sea a great erne dives, snatching.

4

Eventide

Sun slowly sinking above the river rushing,
Lime-white lilies trumpet to the moon aloof,
Fatted fowl wading, an end to days hushed,
Lo, mercurial otter slips downstream—poof!

Song of Spring

The swelling brooks, so clear toned,
Rolling rounds over musical stones,

That unveil the rushed veins of May,
Race in wide cool stills, freshnesses,

Of the moistened soils overturning
And the chimes in the belled leaves,

Before they shout from buds keyed,
To syncopate in sun by bopping bees

Who buzz with jazzy pillowing waft,
Of daisy downs, in midair to reeds,

Lips newly sprouted, banding green,
Groove myriad symphonies of colour

And the roots of trees tempo tapping,
Into waters plucked, earthy sounding,

All voice in joys with woodland birds,
Do trumpet, O what new life to come.

Winter

My window frames me in reflection,
I gaze out to the snowy mountains
Beyond myself, yet before such places
You have run to, it has been so long,
Now comes another new winter, I see
Snow drifts reaching, winds to the sky,
High atop the autumn-white mountains
Paler than loneliness, white as my hair.

Bogman

Ruddy and worn,
Dusted by turf and salt,
Sun rose cheeked and blue
Clouded eye spurt in a gait
Ended by mute journeys and toil.
He breaks the long day with a shove
As the old pocked door is waiting to be
Opened. At the crowning stand of the bar
He orders his Craic, some froth of tar, his black
Medicinal and when the tales of tall pints grow, sinking,
Live, flickering light slows and smoulders, shoulders with moist
Embers of smoke trailing by with an impromptu céilí and all is brilliant,
Blind, awful, and right, cast in the sprite, spirited dance of the verbal swirlings.

Meeting

In a forest clearing deep in wood,

I spied the grace of doe and fawn

And stopped my track as I should,

To set my gate about-face in song.

At Edge of Sea

By the sea, I saunter and think of her,
The tides slip into wild coves—
Like my own desires under moon.

I search the skies, emptiest horizons,
As the gawking gulls circle in windy
Tempests of confusions.

Shy stars appear as the sun is destroyed
And the sea sprays like a bursting fire—
Plastering rocky crags.

The long night that always, was coming,
Has thieved its way from white hope,
A shroud for a sea journey.

A lone osprey shuttles a fish to its nest,
His heart—soaring on high—
While mine submerges at edge of sea.

Walking Flowers

Nature cut her ties,
The stem wanders,
Petals splay in wind,
Woman spreads open,
Man needles so within,
Fruit will come, to drop,
After loves have spoken
And the new walking limbs
Of ripeness that leaves out,
Shall branch into us, light,
Under a sun which seethes,
In the salt of the scorn flesh,
The petals of woman alive,
Such nectar that man must
Halve of himself into world
And kind release, breakings
With water unto high earthly
Being and lands unknown,
Like a Phoenix after ashes,
In a shower of clay, dried
Yet bountiful with bloods
Streaming to the afterdays
Of progeny and old hatch,
To hold with stars as chaos
Falls, seeding casted comes,
Liquids into spinning births.

Irish Sea on the Way to Greystones

We walked along the grainy ocean,
Our way, smooth as a path to nowhere
And through a dance of reeds your hair,
Steeped with marshes of wings and air,
Red, mellow as fire from the fallen sun,
Your flowered dress was the first spring
Ever germinating and blue crystal waters
Sprung, of coastal pools, Knockanare wells
And I was flung, as a windy clutch of seeds
Dreaming, your voice, bloomy, song wafted,
Rousing, as remembrance in fragrances—
And the moony, blinking stars soon peopled
Our woeless eyes, full of sleep and vision
And all the stones held us deep as sarsen.

In Disused Field Is a Blooming Temple

In disused field is a blooming temple.
An ancient apple tree waiting eternal,
This stone-bold sculpture was forged
With nimbus hands and windy eyes.
In hushed airs, Shiva dances to light,
Waves, sacred arms without swaying.

Bearded ones come to pay homage,
The solemn chickadees, the ranging
Sparrows, red-robed robins—priestly
Doves, all who see are one enveloped
In graces of the New World Bodhi tree,
Waiting for blossoms so dearly come.

Edge of boughs brim under heavens
Landing with mystic verges of spirit
Into the mind of the eyes of nature—
Kali-flowered ears of lichen are pale
Green in their devotions, pummeled
By seas of seasons, foggy to the fray.

Finches, yellow, reflecting in a star,
Devout wee lamas golden with halo,
Are kneeling above berm, this knobby
Trunk, stave, inside bodacious stupa
Bell who sings clear, without ringing,
Body of elder grace, wisdoms, ages.

In cast irreverence, seldom do crows
Visit, when they do there is menace
Of the Jinn, dark giants in the levels,
Mercifully, out of shame, they do not
Stay, black wings due, die in luminous
Day moon, rain-soak sun, balmy mist.

On pilgrim journeys, whirlings, prayer
Wheels, guide shy flocks riding gnarl,
Indie goddess, to overreaching love,
By sores of hollow in the steps, open
To being, brindles of myriad meadow
In temple blossoms—numinous suns.

Of both earth and sky, shines a beauty,
Whose form is written in blistering bark,
The ciphers of tongue to Sanskrit leaves
And lost fruits, given over, unforbiddens,
Within old apple tree a great wilderness
And all the branch of wings are knowing.

Wicked

I have come to the temple
Of your body. I kneel and prey
Like a sinner. The holy water
Beads low on your forbidden
Tabernacle, sears my touch
In cleansing flame, what I do
And what will be done is all
For unrepentant confessions
And penances. Let me truly
Learn the sacraments of flesh
Before I bathe in your wicked
Innocence and commit my sin
At being mortal in your nimbus
Chambers, let the mercies rain
After the fall of my fellowing
Creature, for this night is blood
Sabbath, and sacrilege under
A Pagan moon and let the dawn
In the rising sun of mute morning
Be my absolution, our benediction,
Let the moving waters enfold us,
Pure as lambs, as washed babes,
Baptismal.

Veined Wings Fell When I Died

Veined wings fell when I died,
Fell in mid-flight on one last
May Day, on fire with the sun—
Only the dust knew me there,
It fell so gracefully with me.

A downy feather, once was—
Dropped from on high, before
A great white falcon turned the air,
Even thought to prey or of stooping,
Of noble birth was I, falling earthward.

One dry—red, pine needle fell,
Lost in thick piney bed of so many
Others strewn on the forgotten said,
The wind as it unceremoniously fled
And now no path was leading there.

At one grassy edge of a dingle—
Bay some gravel clay gave way
To form a place where water, airy,
Lolls and eddies into tiny whirlpools,
This was all the dance of my days,

Only the dusk knew me there—
And the unobserved eclipse going
Through all its phases and a forest
Fired, under clovers without bees,
Veined wings—fell when I died.

Estranged

Here I tread on a woodland promontory—
With wings and wind conjuring the rains,
All is vastness and shroud, open, empty,
Even the light is carried away in silence,
My flesh all but smearings on the tableau,
Foothold of dream within disrupted dream,
Our hands once reached out into forever,
Now my soul is seeping from veined cairns,
Cut chains, mist, rains hollowing the wind.

Fall of the Wolf

One day gone in the long great forest
Of the ancient world, wolves alone
And mighty hungered with true kin
Stalking the tundras of the snow drifts
And all their prey, with cautionary eyes
Moved in herds and flocks swaying
With the sounds of the forest floor
And the spearing grasses. The wolf
Was his own master, free, unbounded.
A great spirit, brother to the moon.

One dying day, when the bushes burned
They came upon the garbage dumps
Of early man. Their smoke was laden
With the smell of fresh kill, small skins,
Animals, ended trail, and salted death.
Many wolves circled in fear, their pits,
Only one or a few tasted the leftovers,
The easy scraps and bones, tailings,
The elder pack would not stoop for.
These few unguarded wolves morphed
And mated with each other, their mane
And fur, soon was tamed, soon became
Mottled and brown no silver remaining.
This was the fall of the wolf, not man
And the moon turned white, when wolf
Became dog.

Thistles

In gravest, gravels of untouched soil,
Spearhead of purple, beyond the pale,
One statue of siege upon a windy foil,
What mires meek airs in all you survey?

Like a frost of summers, you are lord,
To hold that seed in your spiny face,
Depressions of land your promontory,
All up with arms, ironclad as a mace,

Beneath you, the grown motley fields
Are desolate, all flowers bled, blender,
Spiders and birds know you unyielding,
The lost aleatory scent of no surrender.

Apple and Madrone

In my garden, feral and overgrown,
I bear with branchings of the apple,
Hunched and grey, laden with fallow
Fruits, the tired, knotted fingers die
Each year, under which are baubles
Of sourness and stray, poorly drawn
Circles of fodder even hungry deer
Will not graze upon. The elder tree
Slowly casts itself into bonsai stone.

Down a valley, in the grades of sun,
Lay a stand of madrones in redden
Fire, with deepest eyes of burnished
Green leaves, some immortal Gorgon
So beauteous, in form and branches
Divine, of Olympian flame, held, atop
Heavenly escarpments by the loving
Skies. I see it for what it is, my love,
Your body and hair, so tawny, so fair,
Though, ever lost to me but in dream,
Are dearly those red branches, a fable,
Your eyes, green as sea, those leaves.

Politicians

So many tawdry birds,
Grey, brown, and black,
Suited as they sully in sun,
In feather and windy-speak
And dream, drifting to profit
Points, marring the globe,
They have so many ways
Of singing on their swings
Behind bars, murky birdies,
Gawking in the crowded fields,
Fielding, flighty questions without
Answer, winging all souls to oblivion,
Who fly, flustering, dusting with song,
Twisting the air into pure falsehoods,
Curious, grounded pets for kingdoms,
For masters, fly-hopping in their cages.

Stone Chapel

Frozen in rains, cloistering,
So severe in the dark of day,
Is the walled clutch of garden,
No one escapes, a gilded reaper,
Born of fears, promises beyond,
Of joys on the oak-nailed pews.

Above the lost naves, who stand
In worship to a ghost, bones bent,
There are cast arches of old sorrows,
Veiling the lighted eyes of the cosmos,
Shutting out even mercies, heavenly
Lights duly smoked of incense.

And slated roof, so statuary cold,
Of aged rock and moss under spire,
That even the doves, as they coo
Are grounded, up muted hollows,
Chimes that merely echo guilts,
By shadows of faithless pride.

Forest Gods

I left the house of the tempest brewing,
Spinning like a rod, spun into flame,
And came upon the redwood forest,
Eternal, shouting out heaven's name.

The sun was indifferent, the creek shuffled
Its lament, the birds fluted their dirge—
I was so small, in the red giants' grove,
Yet, felt so beloved, my pain was purged.

And I warmly came to see again—
My eyes, through the needles drove,
What a trifling is one's fleeting mood,
How true, heroic, immortal is my love.

Garden Theology

Adam eyed Eve looking askance,
High in rush of ancient low garden,
Tempted by sun, under all is dance,
Sensate and flesh was torn, bidden.

As stems prickled in moist of garden,
Into dark soils grew blooms of youth,
In rains set free showering new Eden,
The bodies of heaven rose let loosed.

Creation dressed up in their ripeness,
Shouting louder than slithered serpent,
Adam fell drunk under moon of silence,
As Eve, laid down, a star burst bleeding.

Because We Could Not See

Because she could not see—
Song in flower, light in lovers abed,
Dream unfolding as we touched,
Because her great beauty was gifted
It was unfelt, undeserved, shunned,
Making her even more irresistible.

Because I could not hold on to self,
Beside such dream, lost to my hands
As prints clutched into the ruin dark
Of her indifference, I made peace
With subjugation and humilities riven
Out of soul and flesh and hollow being.

Because we were unknowing, each
A foil unto ourselves as we cried—
This then was daymare riding in sun,
Twin delusions in oft reign of blood,
O what stories we both shall die to tell,
How the itch of desire scratches bare
Whole psyche as it writhes in a shell.

Books and Film

In youth, to myself I thought,
"Is true love bound in some faraway place?"
I flew off— picturing dreams to be had.
Ah, so much in books and on film I saw
And so I settled my gaze,
Westward to love.

And I met a girl who knew,
Trades of skin which came and quickly fell,
Of longings true it was not to be had.
Ah, so much in books and on film I saw,
So I left her one glad day,
For we did not love.

O love, so nebulous a thing,
Windings on wheels, windy fates command,
If I could but contain her starry light,
In a wrapped box of hopes, still, on reels,
Recorded in books, in films—fables,
Ah, such an album I would dream.

Then came my only, true one,
The coolest rains held in longest summer,
But soon even bliss in a shower ends
And words to eyes but stories—whims.
Ah, so many pictures I made,
In a camera without film.

Ode to Alleyways

Woe is any town or village
Without alleys. Pathways
Behind the glamour shops
And shut, work-a-day worlds
Of the weary, township mates
Who drown after their labours.

In the small, backyard keeps,
Alleys unhinge the moon's
Sorrows even before great
Mercies, breaks of sun, fall.
Alleys of gravel and earthy
Tar, are as veins communal.

Walk among stillness, only
To know what shines hidden,
See the unkept wild yards,
Bright flowers forsaken, yet
So full of life. Hear new birds
Rehearsing ancient songs
And be glad there is music,
To rouse and uproot a soul,
In the afterthoughts of day.

Death Insinuates as Whisper

Soft is the caul of breaths that seethe,
Loosed in the ears knowing
And light is held as a knife is sheathed,
Hard at the breaks reckoning.

Ebbing crawls in old cradles outset,
Clutched promises engulfing,
Death is a toll which gathers at sunset,
Ending seeps seaward in chills.

Listen for moon as it sails into lime,
Digging lost trails for journey,
Smell the salts as the sands run time,
Boarding penny barks turning.

Black birds soon flutter at drips' window,
When dark winds cry cross-legged,
Lightless wings whisper—lit knowings,
Wraiths tapping three score and ten.

High in Heavens

High atop shining mountains,
Where Gods glint as they spy
On wanting mortals, cast in heat
And toil, in heavens that are always
Basked by sun and days of grape,
That flow from the endless pour
Of golden casks, give mirth to always
Blue veins as they revel in mighty
Perfection and beauty, enameled
With imperishable face and statuary
Form, who thunder above feathery
Cloud, rumbling beyond all earthly
Ken and dream—in these heavens,
Is there myth only of desire?

Or do they yearn in cradle sleep,
As all those landed babes in need
Of mercies and fable, do Gods shape
Subtle creations with the music of love,
Of blood in a touch, of dawn and hope
In the flowering of family and learning?
Can the gleaming child ever know needs
As they are met, held by eyes and lip,
The windy caress of kiss and nod
And rarest time as it wanes?

On radiant, fabled Olympus, where
Eagles, golden in the sun, only rake
The rims of Elysium as they song glide
So effortlessly, unlike the perilous, shy,
Wandering tribes basely set so far below,
The sun-clad Titans' home eternal, who always
Are held, perpetual in ever engulf of skies, rest
Starry, in their sparkling, immortal cloaks
Of milky cosmos and ambrosial aethers.

Above the murmuring clamours
Of the under strays and dogs of plain
And sea, do chose children of light ever
Quake or shudder in awe, never moved,
Or are they but wielders of storm and fierce
Lightning strikes, burnishing in judgment flame,
Never to be struck by leaves that come in fires of autumn,
Such monumental peace in a season's turn, the simple joinings,
Of lovers, by a hearth, by a road, by rush of mountain streams?
In high heavens do even the Gods not dream
Of deep, down, sole earthly pleasures?

Pine Tree

Some branches of broken horn
Called to me, as most others
Were rungs, the trunk, a great pole
For one to vault, into the heavens
Where was perched a wild nest
Of a red-tailed hawk, at the top
I could see the great bird, once
Was there, upon his cloud throne
And all the woods and ripples
With the lake, in dear murmurings
Played for me to soundly hear
The waves lap onto the shores
Under my flight and the lighted
Breeze that sifted through needles
And the sap that patched me there
Out on the limbs of my swaying
Daze.

O to sail in the scented sun
Of the great old pine of tinted
Sage and black tall bark, to be
Nestled in the forests on high
Within its mystery and wisdom,
All the way up I rose, the journey
Earthward was so much harder.

Winter Comes

At first the world, seems on hire,
Threads chill through leaves on fire,

Black ponds grow still under sun,
In opens, slowest silence begun,

Smokey clouds in sweep overlook,
Clime of frosts branched under foot,

Cold winds come and with heaves,
Shattered froze crockery of leaves,

In icy banks bare rivers run out,
Snap as they steam into a knout

And in tawnys of soggy marshes,
Colours grow grey, wet and harsher,

In blisters to come winter shores,
As creatures huddle to frozen floors,

Above are trailings of birds who flee,
Below are underlings rooted in tree,

In sheets of white a graveyard blows,
Black stones piercing the first snows.

In Spring Meadow a New Song Is

In spring meadow a new song is—
Laid on an earthly table with birds
To feather nest, breaths remember,
Budding poems of leaves embrace,
All season is watered, warmly held
Dearly, bright and kept into drying
Bouquets. Little creatures—flutter
In concords, humming with breeze
Caught fallows freed into sanctuary
Of bloom and spark, do clearly note
Abundance soon will break, arrived
To reasons that trail green into fires
Of earned, autumnal transcendence,
The flowers of peak, mature fruition.
In a spring meadow, celebrations all
Thrown—confetti let loose by Gods.

The Ploughman

Still pale grey earth is turned,
Deep is the loam moisted,
Lone by the Ploughman.

The rows of the brushed patches,
Sweating the breakneck blood,
Are painted by labours.

Messiah doors out cathedral,
With iron plod anoints the soil,
Exposed unto mercy sun.

His hands are knobbed in stone,
His eyes searing of the star,
His face dark as deep loam.

Each day ablutions of sod earth,
Heaved out tilling unfree wills,
Burdens of harnessed beast.

Dark is the turned loam moisted,
Water flame heat of veined mist,
Seeds sown explode to bloom.

After thorny works, crowned blood,
Sun leaves to wine-red fruition,
Ploughman maker is done.

Cat and Dove

Mourning dove, set on black wires above
The cool, garden lawn, looks down on cat,
Who is burning blithe birds in greenest eyes,
He tastes them as he chirps in trouncing trance
Fixating upon fixing them, his pious patience
Is Job-like, steadfast, gracious as lifted wings.
Early next day, all that is left of fallen mourning
Dove, is a bed of feathers strewn on the lawn.

The Swans at Dusk

In dusk a cloud moves,
Barely are there any stars
And the sheet drops, sinks,
As lovers we came to this
Gentle pond without guile
Under the willows green,
Set on the banks of whin,
In sight of a stone bridge
And settled in to watch
The swans arrive and go,
Like windy arcs of bounty
Under great falling blanket
Of indigo and gold sparkling,
Enameling eyes of the heavens.

Now, I come to visit alone,
Only memories gliding slow,
Love has fled near after song
The sweetest spring awakening,
How time unveils dark truths,
My hair, it falls in the wind
With the groping willows,
The godly eyes of the skies
Are now mere stars that flash,
My love is betrothed to another,
Still, the cool white swans at dusk
Ride in waters turned shallow, murky
And black as their eyes in day fall,
And yet they remain wondrous,
White rose of my soul,
Drifting away.

Hummingbird

Little king of sun-toasting petal,
Cups the air with swirling wings
Flashes, flurries of wetted trials,
How you drink of nectar singing,

With invisible wings let whirring,
So robed in arc of rainbows' sky,
Even lofted mist of morn stirring,
All the shaped air, a moving eye.

King Lear in Conversation with the Sky

Lear wanders in stormy open, bares warring elements,
The heavens blister, crackle, night is balmy shroud,
Wretched monarch babbles in sprinkles of wind cold,
Arguments lost by one's own pouring perturbations
And raining sky said "nothing will come from nothing."

Howl, howls into blackness treed in lightning splits,
His outcast soul, reels, fleshed, cut to smithereens,
Tang of salt burns on the bluffs and the sea rages,
So entire and ceremonious is Lear's fall meted out,
Air spoke, "nothing from nothings ever yet was born."

Sky proclaimed to man-child King, here is a reckoning,
Each mad choice was self-infliction, now wind flays
And sweet Cordelia lies in her innocent weed grave,
Sky, in thralls of thundering asks, "what say thee now,
King of highborn follies, even purple heaths are rags,

Yet black and above you and night shades, whine,
Unworthy King, done in by compounded effects,
The might of maelstroms in low butterflies' wings,
How now, bare trees, knifing reeds, skeletal flashes,
To rains of night are ever your lanyards my lord."

Sad Lear so near oblivion fell mute, sky went on,
"Howl and cry mad King your reaper calls beyond,
The icy brisk heavens await to brusque you away,
Your slipshod kingdom was mere and fools' dream,
Howl, til howls abrupt abate, for nothing now comes."

Jailbreak Fails

Held in the pens
Of womb, little one
Squirms to see light,
Before the bars of crib
Encroach and bind one
Growing into childhood.
Then to be left off, bounded,
For chaste schools to yearn how
To keep such place whilst learning,
Never knowing that old, bracing sun
Is all around until frightful bell—calls
Recess, for these are the walled gardens
We made for ourselves, the coldest brick
And mortar chambers we place as lambs
Are encased, when finally we are pushed
Into the dark, the drabness, of the drowning
Work a daze whirled, the open prison of our lives.

The Piper

From out of the smoke,
And impromptu silences,
A lone piper plays at reels,
Beyond the borders, his knees
In a trinity of keys, breaching
Low dun-black soused hearts,
The public house is enclosed
Out in the open, under a plow
Of mossy stars, peat and bog,
Wrapped, within chanter's throat.

Glittering Dream

Under fish-scale skies—breaks the sun,
In myriad eyes, beamed longing across
Stupendous arcs in highest procession,
As we make our way in glittering dream.

Under quilted clouds, in rains we swim,
Wrapped in fibers and whim, a webbing
Embrace and steeples of mind to shim,
As we enter the waters from a shooting.

As child we ask, "do we return to whence
We came, or do we end, after days, time,
Thru sorrows and bliss and sleep but lent,
Balm for us to bear loss of spent dream?"

Under winking stars and full-faced moon,
We sing our songs writing a story loosed
And pray our hands, to a feather will turn,
As we make our way thru glittering dream.

By the Druid Stone

I came to a courtyard of my own making,
To a cottage by the sea at the world's edge.
I furnished it with my leftover life, complete,
Barren and colourless and I wrote the newest
Book of psalms out of tinder and flame, a tome
Of grey and useless poems, unheard-of songs
And reams of flesh. There in the lightest dark,
By the Druid stone that was placed just for me,
I planted a creeping yew tree. And the moon
Sang in celebration and silence like a fallen
Priest.
            Under the covering hazel trees,
That sprung to life after the longest winter,
Which taught me to forget my name, I now
Struggle with light and my body, warring, torn
Is fading slow, like the always arriving, down
Turning solstice, the climates of the mind,
Where it is digging the never-ending shallow
Hole only the spreading eternal yew, that I
Planted, will ever know and only the Lazarus
Moon shall ever rise above.

I came to a courtyard of my own making,
Was it dream that led me there or my eyes?

Marrowstone Isle

We drove to a lost, lonely isle,
And where, if only once to find
Ourselves sown again, belonging
Wholly to the keep of faraway strands
That hours tided us in beads and wave,
The nascent sea whispering aloft and birds
Cascading as we flew, to sail under moving
And hoary dunes with stellar eyes of poppies
Wild, such breathtaking strides for we to make
And the sun set dripping and lowly swept ashore
Away to us on breaths of gentle crests breaking,
We spoke sundry nothings, as if to know things
So simple are to be kept wanting nor ever said,
The lonely, dull star of day fell sleepy, dimmed
By sparks, the shimmer to our eyes—

                                        So clear,
Shall be the hills of the fair isle to us, will always
Remain cast with new lamb and crowned deer,
By thorn and thistle and rimmed with broken shells
Rung on marbled beach, singular, before innocence
And grace, by skip-stoned lovers cradled in only sky
To be joined, with the lined hands of long night stars,
Finally reaching in the jeweled glass by the running
Grains polished, a gild castle moat, stained into ocean
Salt, always by the sea of windows' glory and joys given
To each, ever to be thrust upon the high tunes eternal,
Beside the stations of grass and drifted heartwoods,
Among wings by the slip of tides, ripped monumental;

Till when we drove away, this time, in a carriage stall
And all the tumbles of sand into eyes crumbled to end,
We drove ourselves back to riven sleep, a stark beyond
The fallen wayfare columns of momentary paths, we cut
Home, trudging through the garden forests and inlet
Bays on serpentine road, always ever to cross—
A bridge of sighs.

November Gift

The frost, sets in and leaves of red have fallen.
And a cold sun beads on the stiffening ground,
Nimbus clouds, snows of down, now wafted in,
Tagging sun become louder, as ripples on pond
Are waging white with grey, dabbing the tableau,
That nature is painting with a pair of wild swans.

Summer

Our time flicked with drops of summer,
The numberless nodes, mellow cicadas,
Pixelated a world swirling of music—
All dates, sweet tabulations of primes,

The savours swelling in fragrant breeze,
The still waters of pond mist and flame,
How your eyes, with mine, gazed into—
O sleepy windows of eyes being born,

Flowers made a bed and we drank it all,
The light of the sun as it passed in grace
And the birds sang songs of remembrance,
Water fell but once from mothering skies,

Wind whined, such days could never last,
One flesh of burgeoning—moon in the grass.

Anatomy of a Tree

Its form was made for sky,
Reaching into hung heavens.

In the amniotic soils are blood
Veins of bone becoming root.

At the earths breaking is light
Green within the sprouts barking.

To the golden sun on its journey,
The trunks ring into skies praying.

More leaves do come as everlasted
Springs in new revolutions of years.

All the twined branches are knotted
As they grasp the blue firmaments.

And scriptures of heavens proclaim,
Here be journaled leaves, life seeding.

In the Love Field

In the love field are colours at prayer below sun,
The dissipated shades in morning give way—
A hush of dark stamped out for choir that comes,
Each flower sings saviour, each petal a blade.

Happy heads affixed their stalks, free as wind,
Unfurl each day, great vessels, stationary sails,
Louder than any pride could break or cast a sin,
Wild are the flowers that rout, rooting in vales.

In the love field, shadows are writhing with clouds,
Underthings of truthful sun, weightless in the skies,
Pilgrim eyes are watered upon entering this proud
Watercraft of blossom blowing up mad secularity.

To spy upon such sprite loveliness we are lost,
Strangers all, the mindful beauties giving scents,
Luminous pupils tearing high into eyes of gods,
The painted harmonies chime, fixed in the lent,

Tithes of rain and sun shower, raise bloom of tower
Cathedral where dead plains are ribbed from ash
And brazen head of stranger is schooled by flower,
In moments fled from city stalls of steel and glass.

May Flies

In my darkest hour, by the rage of sun,
I met her in a shower of April days,
Riding to the moon in twined études,
The dry chrysalis of winter shells
Gave way to lightness, glaze,
The rain in our eyes, amaze,
Her voice as it fluted, broke,
Like feathers from a wandering bird,
Were my wings of iridescence and joy
And we were blind when we were born,
We were blind as bells of floating grace,
Lived forever by such a new shore,
Such ends of buzzing time,
As May flies.

In Cemetery Lots

The wind carries its soft dirge
Out to sea, across a lamented
Land of bones and vail memory,
Sea birds sail in solitary griefs—
Above the loam that light darkens
As each soot year is lowly churned.

And the slate stones are mossed,
Like trees that no one is hearing,
In forests bereft, unto the shawls
Of ferns as they bleed in the dank
Undergrowths of sorrels and weed
Curling in trite, pale green contritions.

In cemetery lots, the dead are stoned,
Intoxicated on their lost beds of lime,
Where trees surround in wrangled keeps
And bare feets are buried by the spades,
With the untrod grasses, trimmed like nails
And the daisies that rain from the ground.

Drinking Song

Red is my ale,
Like the red of her hair,
Crowds in the pub, shuffle
And dart and all around is merriment,
Looking into my bottomless pint,
Facing the bars closing—
My muted voice mumbles,
Sighs, welled with sinking eyes,
Silent as my prayer.

Night Meadow

Under the primrose stars, the lovers
Lie abed, on green, threadbare croft
Of sleeping daisy, clover, and moss,
Trails with hushed air, an embroidery
So fine as to stitch blushing heart fall
And wrap the waters full of quietude
In graces, winding, soft, granulating
Time, wings flutter and hum, winsome
Sparks, fire white, flying as little suns
Burst confetti, in sweet encampment,
Of grass and sapling wood, innocents,
Charmed are wholly twining, in moon
Rise a lantern to the winking heavens,
Out of their skins they are climbing.

Blake's Moon

In a grove of seven oaks
From my run-down cottage
I see, the night clouds saunter
And drift and spinning round,
The breakneck moon, beaming
With joyous abandon, the piercing,
Painted white face of a pagan God.

Ode to Great Blue Heron

Seasons shuttle the tall stoic figure,
Graceful and solemn as wafted mist,
When seen, as if he was always there,
Overarching into meek, gloamy skies
Of mornings and dusk, midday, lost,
Seems not right for wading out kills
That crane from above into the mud
And murk of the penny-eyed waters
Only the ferryman will tender, for time
Slips, sleeping with the fishes, spears
Puddle and rim in the wakes, sparks
Of waters break like a sputtering fire,
His dart eyes are as yellow as golden
Sun dancing in funeral pyre. So green
Creatures, must they always be gotten,
Gone, have it coming from the sheering,
Mercies of the Great Blue Heron who is all
Seeing, scything, down to dazed judgment,
Incited, pecking to order at the squirming fold.

Old Tree in the Sun

Grasping to the sky
With ever-reaching
Branches, leaves spirit
Themselves to sacred airs.

Old tree, a star set
Truncated with sprite earth,
Stolid, touchstone spark,
Place, feeling all waves
Dripping by like clouds.

In some underworld,
Bathing with Gods,
Are immortal roots
Divining water, laid
In ceremonious soil,
Digging out golden,
Unfallowed tombs.

Old tree in the sun,
Great soul barking
Skywards each day,
Joyous arms clench,
Lancing, higher out,
Embracing heavens.

As Embers Preen

*"If the doors of perception were cleansed, everything would
appear to man as it is—infinite."*

—William Blake

In this room
Drowning,
In ocean flesh,
Our days, replay,
With eyes cut
Out under sheet
Of stars. All is
Not real, screened
For a soul, lost
On the dry lands
We bury ourselves
In.

    One day we shall
Wake into the sun,
And bathe in the light
Of unbridled constellation
And voids deeper than
Life, holy and actual
Like drowning flesh,
Come, alive in sky,
Lit by eternal sheen,
Lost memories, grace,
Being burn, new sparkle,
Cast to air, as embers preen.

Early Spring Morning

Light sparkles in the clover,
Yellow and blur of bees
Are honeyed in the sun
And robins have come,
Yanking in the grasses,
So green is the moisten
Of the painting of the dew
And all is lolling in petrichor,
The soils running with slow
Time so shortly experienced,
Oils of wood permeate the air,
Lapping brooks bream into light,
The loft kestrel swirls in meadow
And chipmunks scuttle at base of tree,
Even the wind does freshly quiet, crisply,
There as a hug waiting for body and spirit,
Patches of white are disappearing, they know—
That one day we must all return, after winter snows.

Winter Pass Over

Light
Enamels the naked
Trunks, cleansing
Sun strikes

The unraveled trees
Bolted to frozen ground
And the leaves
Mosaic,

As any temple
Floor, iconic,
Pray, tell stories
Of turned seasons.

In winter
Snows come merely
To raw, all unwashed
And drape purity,

White as truth
And sparse is song
From only the most
Devout birds

Who with hymn,
In the piped choirs
Of icicles, drip
Drop to blessed waters,

Anointing the soiled
Sinner ground,
Waiting for spring
Eternal.

O What Kingdoms

Deep in a garden I lay,
As when before—a world I had made,

I was born on wooded shores,
When sounds of the forest stood calling

And all that day of my youth—
I combed with branches pointing anew,

Grasses, green took to flame
And timber—tall, called out my name,

As a winged seed I spun afar,
Which led me to dreams new under stars,

Wildflowers I left unpicked—
Have painted true my world ever since,

All my time spent—sun raining,
O what kingdoms a child can make.

Providence in the Wood

Rain dapples in fens of the marshland brooks,
Among the rue hillocks of the sapling woods,

What little peace may fall to drop the shivering
Leaves, rood of the sun, a crop, kestrels quiver

In midair, to keep as they sway into the stations
Of all minions moused who falter in formation

And bright is birth, when night clothes the day,
As all the mornings long, song of hope, in May.

Sentinels

Poppies, wild in a quarry,
Orange, brighter than sun,
Thrusting thoroughly gravel,
Bold as soul crossing sticks
Into bloody pagan heydays,
A crop of colours branding
The loose stipend of stones,
One windy trail-flare shock,
A bulwark of stars, so laden
On landed, maiden shores,
The first battalion breaking,
By mighty petal, prim hands
Fiercely alive atop the lifeless,
Gravely low, defeated soot.

The Falcon

Falcon rise—yellow racing eyes,
Blue wraith that rakes the skies,
Never has one fared such beauty,
Airs naught wholly bright as thee.

Is there a kneel for end of days—
Songs, deeds for those who prey?
Is there light breaking pied wings,
Or is heaven overlord to all things?

Sun spots feathering coated crest,
Talons top spires mountain breast,
When rivers of the wind fail all fowl,
What grace and splendour in a cowl?

Is there a psalm in the wailing winds,
A hymn that carries all innocent sins,
Or a fable, blue as stupendous skies,
A truest place where redemption lies?

The sea slides with lost ocean birds
And blue wings coast, row unheard,
Edging the skies with razor's tinge,
Seeding the immortal spark begins.

Falcon rise—yellow racing eyes,
Blue wraith that rakes the skies,
Never has one fared such beauty,
Naught airs wholly bright as thee.

—after William Blake

From the Sky

The sea is a landing,
The mountains, but ribs,
Merely brittle, sandy mounds,
That cradle and rock, my song,
The oceans, bathwater foaming,
My body is all encompassed
In void, in elements of feather,
Light as the rays from the stars,
The Great Lakes are puddles,
And all bands of the ancient
Forest are wrapped in a ball,
The world is a playful bubble,
Only one note from the music
Of the spheres, a loosed bauble
Born of sparks, cosmic clouds,
Breaking in the nebulas of blistering
Iris, exploding in the joyous eyes
Of a waking child.

               Yet, there is only
Now, I am, locked in a dream-house,
By a vast sea, on old branches of tree,
And, I can only look, grow, daze into
Shut mystic heavens, and wonder.
Can I truly, only, live in dream?
My makeshift world is drying,
I am from sprinkled waters
Dropped like tears,
Graces that fell
From the sky.

Deep in the Wood

Good deer are gracing the trees,
Take communion in handed leaf,
Touch the soils with loving hoof,
In the tabernacles of the wood.

The owl cries for all souls eternal,
Deep in the shrouds of the vernal
That drape the newly born dying,
Beneath the solemn owls' crying.

And songbird has a psalm unread,
A parable in the twining branches,
Gifts of song foist lanyards of crop
Dear in old forest, this offered sup.

As blood seeping deep in the wood,
Sky washes away those who stood.

In the Marshes of Youth

We stalked and ran with endless time,
Knee deep in rains of muck, grew lost
In tails of the always new, overreached
By trammeled spots, dotting, red wings
From black birds, knobby toads, garter
Snakes that shocked, marigold swamp
And we bolted above ruddy moccasins,
As ever wet, holey, dying for new days,
Gleaming in the swelters of the horse-
Fly sun, in the giants' grasses, we were
Heroes by the falls of light, glow, dusky
Bold, joys travail and dewy eyes echoed
With sprite flashes by the flies that fired.
And all our conquests—writ in the wind.

Love Out of Touch

Love out of touch, we could not bare
Alone, with loosed arms overreaching
And love sparkled dancing,
On the breaking rim of a star,
Innocent and new under the constellations
Of the pinned gods' eyes.

We told ourselves the story of ourselves,
Each one, a penned, perfect fable,
Each one a journey into the dark,
Under the faint and rising milky ways,
Where even shadows, poor,
Are always, almost, lost.

Out of conception, and pining dream
And the myths we most want to make,
Out of dream, would we soon awaken?

This then is hope, a stroke, as we dressed,
Children spinning yarns below the stars,
Is the game, the game of let's pretend.

We would not bare, love out of touch.

Epitaph in Stone

Something beyond,
To climb into cloud,
Into the snows of purity,
To touch the rise of sun,
Golden as it bathes us,
To realize all is small
Underneath, and all
Is washed by streams
Of blood from the skies,
To reach the highlands,
Plateaus in the heavens,
This is the only poem,
A great blue mountain,
Something beyond,
For us to climb.

Gentle House, Willoughby-upon-Salish-Sea, Cascadia, Washington

Acknowledgments

Acknowledgments are due to the following: *Agenda Magazine, Anagram, Art and Earth, Contemporary Poetry Review, Coracle, Intervention Magazine, Irish Literary Supplement, The London Magazine, Lumpy Pudding Magazine, The Lyric Magazine, New Pegasus, Poetry Ireland, Poet Lore, Poetry Magazine, Poets Online, Romenu Magazine, Stand Magazine.*

"Night Meadow" (sonnet and choral music) was The Uncommon Music Festival winner, 2018 Composer Competition (music by Carlos Cordero; poem by Seán Mac Falls).

About The Author

Seán Mac Falls was born in Boston and grew up in the rural New England townlet of Canton, Norfolk County, Massachusetts, on the shores of his beloved Bolivar Pond. For much of his youth he was a songwriter in Los Angeles, and traveled widely, visiting over thirty countries. He moved to Shankill, Ireland, in 1993, studied Irish literature and folklore in Dublin, and is a dual citizen of Ireland/America. He has written seven collections of poetry: *20 Poems*, *The Blue Falcon*, *iKu*, *Moon Harvest Under Wood*, *Fables and Whim*, *Love Songs of Skye*, and *Garden Theology*. He now lives in Port Angeles, Washington.

Praise for Seán Mac Falls

"In an age of prosaic verse, he [Mac Falls] uses a more charged and resonant language . . . bardic."

—RICHARD WILBUR, former U.S. Poet Laureate

"Seán Mac Falls is an authentic poet. His voice is his own, and his fusion of Gaelic and North American traditions is refreshingly unfashionable."

—HAROLD BLOOM

"I was stirred and cheered by the vigour of them [*20 Poems*]. Whitman seems to be among his ancestors, as well as Yeats."

—JOHN CAREY, Merton Professor of English, Oxford, also critic, *Sunday Times* (London)

"'An ocean of bloom in all direction winked' about sums it up. I admire above all else in poetry that energy and discipline which knows no words can answer to the world but goes on trying anyway. Hopkins had it, and Dylan Thomas, too, and he [Mac Falls] has it."

—THEO DORGAN, former director of Poetry Ireland

COLOPHON

A Note on the Typeface

THE text is set in Golden Cockerel, a typeface created in 1929 especially for the Golden Cockerel Press. It is part of the Perpetua family of fonts, designed by the English sculptor, calligrapher, and woodcut engraver Eric Gill (1882–1940), mainly identified with the Arts and Crafts Movement. Perpetua is often classified as a transitional serif font, with a delicate structure somewhat similar to British fonts from the eighteenth century such as Baskerville and stone-carved inscriptions in the same style. Perpetua's appeal to fine book printers has been long-standing since its release, both in the UK and abroad.

The Golden Cockerel Press is one of the most outstanding private presses of the twentieth century. The press was a highly creative environment, working with poets, writers, and artists. It was set up in southern England in 1920 by a cooperative of four inspired but inexperienced partners in a small village in the Berkshire countryside. Their venture struggled and grew into a press that is renowned for producing some of the most beautiful handmade limited-edition books of the twentieth century—now much sought after by collectors. Eric Gill worked closely with Robert Gibbings in the 1920s developing his ideas on typography and book design.